Vanishing

Forests

Lim Cheng Puay

Raintree
Chicago, Illinois

First published in North America in 2004 by
Raintree, a division of Reed Elsevier, Inc.
Chicago, Il 60602
Customer Service 888-363-4266
Visit our website at www.raintreelibrary.com

For more information address the publisher:
Raintree, 100 N. LaSalle, Suite 1200, Chicago Il 60602

Printed and bound in Malaysia

08 07 06 05 04
10 9 8 7 6 5 4 3 2 1

© 2004 TIMES MEDIA PRIVATE LIMITED
Series originated and designed by
Times Media Private Limited
A member of the Times Publishing Group
1 New Industrial Road, Singapore 536196

Co-ordinating Editor: Isabel Thomas
Writer: Lim Cheng Puay
Series Editor: Katharine Brown
Project Editor: Katharine Brown
Series Designer: Lynn Chin Nyuk Ling
Series Picture Researchers : Susan Jane Manuel, Thomas Khoo

Library of Congress Cataloging-in-Publication Data
A copy of the cataloging-in-publication data for this title is on file with the Library of Congress.

ISBN: 0-7398-7012-2

The publishers would like to thank the following for permission to reproduce photographs:
• Cover: Photodisc (top), Still Pictures (main) • Title page: Art Directors and Trip Photo Library • Imprint page: Art Directors and Trip Photo Library, Photodisc, Corel, Living Heritage Trust of Sri Lanka (left to right) • AFP: 44 (bottom) • Art Directors and Trip Photo Library: 4, 6, 8, 9 (bottom), 11 (top), 12, 13 (top), 14 (top), 24, 25 (bottom), 27 (bottom), 29 (both), 32, 38 (top) • Bes Stock: 9 (top), 15 (top) • Camera Press: 17 (bottom), 18 (top) • Corbis: 13 (bottom), 36 • Corel: 5, 11 (bottom), 25 (top), 30, 31 (both) • Forest Stewardship Council: 44 (top) • Fotomedia: 41 (top) • Houserstock Inc.: 28 • Hutchison Library: 21, 23 (top) • Joginder Chawla: 40 • Living Heritage Trust of Sri Lanka: 35 (bottom) • Lonely Planet Images: 18 (bottom), 20, 34, 37 (bottom), 38 (bottom), 39 (both), 43 (bottom) • Mirelle Vautier of Paris: 17 (top) • Photodisc: 7, 10, 14 (bottom), 15 (bottom), 22, 23 (bottom), 27 (top), 35 (top) • Science Photo Library: 19, 43 (top) • S. I. Ahmed 41 (bottom) • Still Pictures: 33 (both), 37 (top) • Topham/Imageworks: 42 • Topham/UNEP: 16 • Travel Ink: 26 • UNEP/Still Pictures: 45

The publishers would like to thank Eric L. Peters, Professor of Ecology and Environmental Science at Chicago State University, for his assistance in the preparation of this book.

Every effort has been made to contact the copyright holders of any material reproduced in this book. Any omissions will be rectified in subsequent printings if notice is given to the publishers.

Contents

Words that appear in the glossary are printed in bold, **like this,** the first time they occur in the text.

Earth's Forests

Forests are places where thousands of trees have been growing together for many centuries. There are different types of forests, depending on the temperature and amount of rainfall they get. For example, trees such as pines and redwoods flourish in the **temperate** regions of North America, Canada, and Europe, while rainforests are found in the tropical areas of South America, Africa, and Southeast Asia.

By fall, most of the trees in this forest in Surrey in Great Britain will have shed their leaves.

Deciduous forests

Deciduous forests are found mainly in North America, South America, Europe, Asia, Australia, and New Zealand. They grow in places with mild winters and warm, wet summers. Each year, these forests receive about 3 to 6 inches (80 to 160 millimeters) of rainfall. Broad-leaved, deciduous trees such as oak, hickory, maple, ash, and beech grow there. Just before winter arrives, deciduous forests become very colorful as the leaves turn red, orange, yellow, or brown. They fall to the ground when the weather gets colder and drier.

Coniferous forests

Unlike deciduous trees, **coniferous** trees do not shed their leaves in winter, so they are also known as **evergreen** trees. The most common types of coniferous trees are pine, fir, and spruce. Coniferous forests can be found in North America and South America, Canada, Europe, and East Asia. Boreal or taiga forests are coniferous forests found in North America, Scandinavia, and the northern-most parts of Europe and Asia. The mountain coniferous forests and pine forests in the southeast regions of the United States are also boreal forests. These places have long, cold winters and cool, short summers. The average temperature is only about 50 °F (10 °C). The plants there have very little time to grow as they can only do so when there is sunlight available.

A spruce tree in a forest in northern Alberta in west central Canada.

Rainforests

Rainforests are probably the most fascinating and important forests of all. They are found in the lush tropics where it is warm and wet all year. At least 50 percent of all the known plant and animal species in the world live in rainforests. Rainforest trees need plenty of rain and constant sunlight in order to grow well. These conditions are only found in parts of South and Central America, Africa, and Southeast Asia. In these areas, the daily temperature is about 82 °F (28 °C) and the average daily rainfall is 0.2 inches (5.5 millimeters). There are up to 1,000 species of rainforest trees, including mahogany and rosewood. Some rainforest trees lose their leaves annually but as they do so at different times of the year, the forest appears to be evergreen.

Distribution map showing the three main types of forests on Earth. The uncolored areas include deserts and grasslands.

Key

- Deciduous forest
- Coniferous forest
- Rainforest

Life Cycle of a Forest

A forest tree starts life as a seed in the ground. The seed could have been blown there by the wind or brought by small animals or birds that ate the fruits of the parent tree. The seed lies **dormant** until there is enough warmth and water for it to **germinate.** When the environmental conditions are suitable, the seedling will emerge from the ground and a pair of small leaves will unfold to absorb sunlight, so **photosynthesis** can start. The forest is a crowded place and many tall trees cover the sky, so the young tree only grows to about 10 feet (3 meters) in height.

Light helps plants grow

The young tree, or sapling, could wait for years until one of the trees near it falls down. When this happens, a **gap** is formed. Sunlight pours in and the young tree starts growing very quickly. Within a few years, it will reach the height of the other trees. The mature tree bears flowers and fruit and produces seeds. When the tree dies, either from old age, disease, or a violent storm, it falls to the ground. The gap it creates allows other saplings to take its place. Fungi and insects called termites break the wood down into smaller, simpler substances. Most of the tree is then returned to the ground as **nutrients** to nourish other trees.

Young and mature cedar trees grow side by side in Lebanon. Cedar trees can grow up to 79 feet (24 meters).

Origins of forests

Long ago, the land where a forest now stands was bare and empty or just simple grassland. Scientists have discovered a pattern to how the plants in a landscape change. Starting from a bare patch of land, the first group of plants to grow will be mosses and small, simple **herbs.** As these plants grow and die, more soil will gradually build up and attract insects and other animals to live in the area. Seeds from other plants will be brought in by these animals or the wind. Slowly the landscape will change as more and more plants grow. The plant species that grow there will also become bigger. Eventually, after many hundreds of years, a forest will form.

A sprouting seedling. Green plants and trees produce **chlorophyll,** *so they can make their own food.*

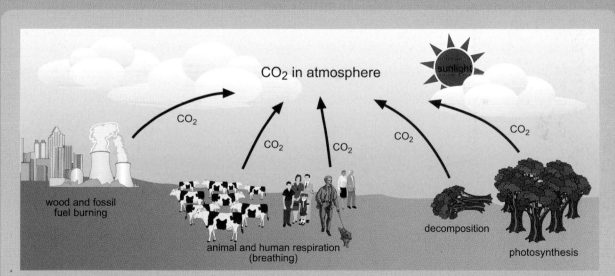

The carbon cycle

Forests play a vital part in controlling the amount of carbon dioxide (CO_2) in Earth's atmosphere. CO_2 is a greenhouse gas, which means it can add to **global warming.** Trees take in CO_2 and give out oxygen (O_2) as they photosynthesize. An average tree takes in 26 pounds (11.79 kilograms) of CO_2 a year and gives out enough O_2 to keep four people breathing.

Forests are a major carbon store. Growing trees take carbon in the form of CO_2 from the atmosphere to make carbohydrates, fats, and proteins. When forests are cleared and the trees rot or are burned, this carbon is released as CO_2. This increases the amount of CO_2 in the atmosphere.

What Is Deforestation?

Deforestation, or the removal of forests, is a major problem that has devastating effects all over the world. Europeans began clearing forests more than 500 years ago. The invention of modern machinery made the process even easier. By the end of the 19th century, most of the deciduous forests of North America, Australia, and New Zealand had been cleared. In the 21st century, tropical forests are being cut and burned at alarming rates in South America and Southeast Asia. Asia as a whole has already lost about 90 percent of its forests.

Forests are home to most of the species of plants and animals on Earth. As forests are destroyed, an estimated 50,000 species die out a year. Pictures taken from space show how the rich **biodiversity** of the rainforest is being replaced with large areas planted with just one crop.

Much of Scotland's forest has been cut down for firewood or to clear the land for agriculture. Forests are believed to have covered about 80 percent of Scotland 2,000 years ago. Today forested areas cover only 2 percent of the land.

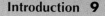

The heavy machinery used to remove felled trees from a forest can damage the surrounding forested land.

Why are trees being cut down?

Forests are mostly cut down to clear the land for farming or grazing cattle. Some local farmers cut trees down and burn them to prepare the land for growing crops, such as rice. Big commercial companies clear large areas of forest to rear cattle for beef. They also cut down many thousands of trees to sell as timber or as wood pulp to make paper. As countries become more developed, demand for these products will go up.

How fast are the forests disappearing?

About 4.3 million square feet (400,000 square meters) of Earth's forests are cleared every minute. That is about the size of 57 soccer fields. In a day, an area the size of New York City disappears. Every year, 81,000 square miles (210,000 square kilometers) of forest are cleared, an area larger than Poland.

Many trees are being cut down in the Democratic Republic of the Congo due to the need for more fuelwood and land for farming.

Tools of destruction

In the past, forests were cleared by hand, using handsaws, axes, or machetes. This involved hard, physical work and was quite slow. Modern machines can clear forests very quickly. A chainsaw can cut down, in a few minutes, a 98-foot-tall (30-meter-tall) tree that has been around for hundreds of years.

Measuring Deforestation

As we depend so heavily on forests, it is very important to know how many there are and how fast they are disappearing. This allows scientists to think of ways to restore the forests or cause less damage while logging. There are several ways that scientists can track how much logging and deforestation is going on. Since vast areas are affected by deforestation, satellites and airplanes can help.

Using satellites

A satellite is an object that orbits Earth. Satellites in space can transmit information, including photographs, to computers on the ground. Scientists use satellites to take pictures of forests around the world. By regularly measuring the area of forested land, they can tell how fast forests are disappearing. Some satellites have special cameras that show heat, so scientists can tell immediately if a forest is on fire.

Using airplanes and aerial photographs

A cheaper and easier way to **monitor** deforestation is to fly over forests to see what is happening. With an accurate map, scientists can see how much of a forest is cut down in a day and estimate the area removed over a period of time. More often, small remote-control planes fitted with cameras are sent to take aerial photographs of the forest. This method uses less fuel and saves time. Aerial photographs show the amount of forest cover in more detail than satellite photographs.

Airplanes like this one are used by scientists to help them see the rate at which forests are disappearing.

A surveyor uses a theodolite to map out eucalyptus woodland in the Northern Territory in Australia. Surveyors also use theodolites to measure how flat land is.

Land surveys

As well as the size of a forest, it is important to know what plants and animals live there. **Indicator species** are animals and plants that show how clean and healthy a forest is. It is impossible to survey every square foot of every forest, so scientists study several **plots** that are chosen at random. They note the different plant and animal species and the numbers of each species in the plot. From these figures, especially the number of indicator species in a given area, scientists can tell how well the forest is coping with deforestation. In other cases, scientists will compare the number of plants and animals in different forests. Less disturbed forests generally have more plants and animals.

Using birds

Birds like the common troupial (*right*) are excellent indicator species because they respond quickly to changes in their habitat. When sections of forest are cleared, the bird species living there have smaller nesting grounds and fewer sources of food. As a result, they fly to other undisturbed forested areas. Biologists and conservationists see the decline in the number of bird species in a forest as a sign of the forest's deteriorating state. **Migratory** birds are also good indicator species. If they return to the same forest year after year, it usually means the forest is healthy.

Agricultural Activities

For many hundreds of years, we have depended on agriculture to feed growing populations. For agriculture to take place, land has to be converted to farms and ranches. Often, large areas of forest are cleared for this purpose.

Shifting agriculture — clearing the land to grow crops

People need land to grow crops like rice and sweet potatoes to feed their families. They often clear forests to get this land. To clear forests quickly and easily, farmers use the slash-and-burn method. A patch of forest is cut down and the trees are burned to release all their trapped nutrients into the soil. The farmers then plant crops. The land gradually becomes **infertile** as the nutrients in the soil are quickly used up. After two to three years, the land is abandoned and the farmers shift to another patch of forest. This method of clearing and moving on is known as shifting agriculture. In the past, this method worked well because each patch of forest was given enough time (20 to 30 years) to grow back. Now, with more and more people using the slash-and-burn method, the land is not given enough time to rest.

Women rest on a log after this section of forest in southern Sumatra, Indonesia, has been cut down and burned. The Indonesian government banned the slash-and-burn method in 1999. Many farmers continue to use this method, however, because it is a cheap way to clear land.

Growing crops for money

Forests are also cleared by farmers to grow crops such as sugar, corn, and soybeans. These crops are sold for money and are a major source of income for a developing country. Many farmers grow coffee to sell to developed countries. At present, coffee farms cover over 12,000 square miles (30,000 square kilometers) of land in the northern parts of South America. Although the coffee industry is booming, the price of coffee beans is falling. Therefore, farmers who grow coffee beans have to plant more for the same income. As a result, more forests are cleared.

Forested land on Saint Kitts in the Caribbean that has been cleared to grow sugar cane. Today more than 50 percent of forests worldwide are under threat of being cleared for farming.

Cattle ranching

The average person living in the U.S. or Europe eats about 64 pounds (29 kilograms) of beef a year. One of the largest **exporters** of beef is Brazil, which is also one of the few places where large rainforests still remain. Brazil exports about 1.1 million tons of beef each year, earning about $1 billion. Large cattle ranches are created by clearing the rainforests, as this is the only land available. The building of cattle ranches now contributes to about 80 percent of rainforest destruction in Brazil. For every pound (0.45 kilograms) of beef a person eats, about 54 square feet (5 square meters) of rainforest are destroyed.

*Cattle ranches also damage the forest in other ways. When the cattle move around to look for food, their hooves **compact** the soil. Rain water cannot seep through compacted soil, so the land eventually becomes unsuitable for forest plants to grow on. After a few years, the soil cannot support plant life any longer and becomes a wasteland.*

Planted forests

Thousands of miles of land in countries such as South Africa and Chile are being planted with trees to supply the paper industry with wood pulp. Unlike natural forests, however, planted forests contain just one or two fast-growing species, usually pine or eucalyptus. These forests have a negative impact on the environment as they use huge quantities of water and reduce the quality of the soil. Also, plants and animals that once lived in the region find it almost impossible to survive in planted forests. Local people suffer, too. As planted forests provide very few jobs, these people have to move to the cities to make a living.

Commercial Logging

A timber plant in Buenos Aires, Argentina. About 53 billion cubic feet of wood is harvested worldwide every year for timber and to provide wood pulp for paper.

When you look around your home, school, and neighborhood, you will see many things made from wood: houses, furniture, and even the pages of this book. Many timber companies are logging tropical hardwoods like teak, mahogany, and rosewood to make furniture, building materials, charcoal, and other wood products. Forests are also cut down for fuel. Two billion people in developing countries, about a third of the world's population, depend on wood as a fuel for cooking and heating.

A logger uses a chainsaw to cut down a tree.

Uncontrolled logging is bad for forests

Logging is a major reason why forests are disappearing so rapidly. When the trees in a forest are cut down, smaller plants grow and take over the land. The forest formed from these plants is known as a **secondary forest.** The biodiversity of secondary forests is not as great as in **primary forests** and the trees, being smaller, are of no value as timber. Also, when trees are felled, their roots no longer hold the soil together. This results in soil erosion.

Other trees are also affected

When a selected tree is cut down, it usually drags or knocks down other trees. As a result, many more trees fall during a logging project than are needed by the lumber company. Even more trees are cut down to make way for roads to carry the timber away. These roads reduce the size of the forest and break it up into smaller areas. This breakup of land is known as fragmentation. If forested areas become fragmented, many animal species cannot survive as they no longer have a suitable or large enough place to live. Roads also make it easier for slash-and-burn farmers to move in.

A truckload of logs being transported out of a forest on Vancouver Island, Canada. About 75 percent of the ancient forests on Vancouver Island have been logged over the past 150 years.

Logging affects rivers as well

Sometimes trees fall into rivers or block up streams during logging. This changes the flow of water, causing some parts of the forest to become dry and other parts to become waterlogged and swampy. This affects trees and parts of the forest that might be far away from the logging area itself.

*Timber and logging companies sometimes use rivers to transport the timber to timber plants. River logging, however, can affect the habitat of aquatic species such as salmon as it can increase the flow of the river and the amount of **sediment** that is washed into the river.*

Soil erosion

Soil erosion happens when soil is washed or blown away by rain and wind. Trees help to prevent soil erosion by protecting the land from wind. Their roots help to hold the soil in place so that it is not easily washed away. When a forest is **clear-cut,** the **topsoil** that contains nutrients can be washed away and the area may soon become a wasteland.

Urbanization

Urbanization is the change from a rural landscape to that of a town or city, which has buildings made from concrete, wide tarred roads, electricity, piped water, and few green spaces. Many people are attracted to city life and they can often make a better living there. Cities provide many comforts and services, including a better choice of schools, hospitals, and entertainment, clean water, and, often, a comfortable place to live. As a result, urbanization is happening at a rapid rate everywhere. The spread of cities into the countryside and rural areas is called urban sprawl.

Clearing forests to expand cities

Forests are being cleared all over the world to make space for homes, roads, and factories. In some countries, nearly all the natural forests have been cut down for building and urbanization. In most of the United States, only 1 to 2 percent of the original forests remain. Another 20,000 square miles (50,000 square kilometers) of forest are expected to be lost soon to urban sprawl in the southern states of the U.S. A similar development is also taking place in the forests of Europe. Tropical rainforests, perhaps the most important forests, are also disappearing at an alarming rate.

This section of rainforest has been cleared to make way for a housing estate in Malaysia.

The land around the city

Cities are not just made up of buildings and roads. They need electricity and a constant supply of fresh water. Once again, land and fuel are needed to provide these facilities, which means clearing more forests. Mining, industrial development, and the building of reservoirs or dams also often result in deforestation.

A mining plant in Carajas, Brazil. Brazil has one of the world's largest reserves of iron ore. As a result, vast areas of rainforest are cleared each year for mining.

Pollution and forests

Factories, power stations, and cars release polluting chemicals into the atmosphere. Some of these, particularly sulfur dioxide and nitrous oxides, dissolve in rain water to produce **acid rain.** When this falls on forests, it damages the leaves or needles of trees and makes the soil so **acidic** that trees eventually die. In the United States, about two-thirds of the sulfur dioxide in the air comes from coal-fired power stations.

Acid rain has destroyed much of the forest in the Izerskie Mountains in Poland.

Dams

More than 40,000 large dams, all over 50 feet (15 meters) high, are currently obstructing the world's rivers. The reservoirs created by these dams cover more than 155,000 square miles (400,000 square kilometers) of land, almost the total land area of Sweden. These reservoirs have flooded thousands of miles of forest, particularly in the tropics. In many cases, the forest trees were not even logged but were left to rot slowly. Conservationists estimate that the proposed Bakun Dam in Sarawak, Malaysia, would involve flooding an area the size of Singapore.

Natural Causes

Though recent deforestation has mostly been caused by human activities, forests also disappear through natural causes. Forests do not last forever even when they are untouched by humans. Other forces, such as forest fires, violent storms, and disease, can also kill trees and cause deforestation.

Right: This tree has been struck by lightning. Lightning can ignite a tree and set nearby trees and shrubs on fire as well.

A fire spreads through Kruger National Park in South Africa.

Fire

Every year, as much as 20,000 square miles (50,000 square kilometers) of forest is destroyed by forest fires, which may have been started by natural factors or by humans. Fires happen frequently in forests during dry seasons when it is hotter and there is little rain. The dry twigs and leaves that accumulate in the forest during that period also increase the risk of fire. A spontaneous combustion, where dry vegetation bursts into flames without any outside heat source, or lightning can trigger forest fires. Lightning tends to strike tall, pointed objects, so trees are at risk because of their height. The heat from a lightning bolt can reach up to 50,000 °F (27,000 °C), over four times hotter than the surface of the Sun. This powerful dose of energy is enough to ignite a tree.

Storm damage

Severe storms can also cause huge damage to a forest. Gusts of wind reaching speeds of over 100 miles (160 kilometers) an hour are strong enough to uproot trees and even clear away entire stretches of forest. A hurricane is a very powerful storm with wind speeds of 75 miles (120 kilometers) an hour or more. Hurricane Hugo is one example of how much damage a big storm can do. In 1989, Hurricane Hugo passed though South Carolina with winds of 121 miles (195 kilometers) an hour. The massive winds destroyed over one-third, or 7,000 square miles (18,000 square kilometers), of the state's forests.

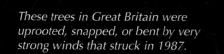

These trees in Great Britain were uprooted, snapped, or bent by very strong winds that struck in 1987.

Plant diseases

Like animals, plants sometimes become sick. If the disease is not serious, they will recover. Otherwise, they will die. Plant diseases can be transmitted from one plant to another by insects, water, or even wind, so it is possible for an entire stretch of forest to become diseased and for all the trees in the area to die. Many trees have been killed by Dutch Elm disease, which is a fungal infection carried by the elm bark beetle. The disease was first discovered in the Netherlands in the 1930s and found its way to the United States, where it has since destroyed over half the elm trees in the northern part of the country. Other plant diseases include fire blight, crown gall, and oak wilt.

Insects may destroy forests

All the animals living in forests rely on plants for food. Insects such as the forest tent caterpillar, the caterpillar of the gypsy moth, and the birch leaf miner may eat as much as 15 million square feet (1.4 million square meters) of forest a year. Gypsy moths were introduced into the United States in 1869 to set up a silk industry. The moths quickly escaped into the wild and are now a major pest. Gypsy moth caterpillars prefer the leaves of deciduous hardwoods such as oak and maple but will also attack evergreens like pine and spruce.

Deforestation and Ecosystems

Deforestation interrupts forest **ecosystems.** Without plants to eat and trees to live in, small animals die and the larger animals that feed on them will also be at risk. Trees take hundreds of years to grow. Once they are cut down, it takes a long time for the forest to recover. More often than not, other types of forests will take over and the original forest may never have a chance to grow back.

Trees are vital to the forest

Trees are the foundation of any forest. In the rainforest, for example, the great towering branches form a **canopy** that acts like the roof of a house. It makes the interior of the forest shady and traps water vapor to make the air warm and damp (humid). Animals living in the forest get their shelter and food from the plants. In return, animals **pollinate** the plants, disperse their seeds, and **decompose** dead wood to return nutrients to the soil.

Rainforest vegetation along the Zambezi River in Zambia.

By 2002, 6 percent of the Brazilian Amazon rainforest had been cut down. But the fragmentation caused by roads and logging sites increased the edge effect and affected an additional 10 percent of the forest.

Forest fragmentation and the edge effect

At the edge of a rainforest, more sunlight passes through the canopy, so it is drier and hotter than the interior. Fewer forest plants grow at the edge because they prefer the humid and shady forest interior. As a result, there are fewer animals there. This is known as the edge effect. Cutting down parts of a forest or building roads through it increases the edge effect. Imagine taking a piece of paper and cutting it up into several smaller pieces. The roads behave like a giant pair of scissors, cutting the forest into smaller fragments. The edge effect can extend some 300 to 600 feet (100 to 200 meters) into the forest.

Deforestation and the climate

Forests are very important to the world's climate because they help in rain formation and absorb carbon dioxide (CO_2) from the air. As the forests disappear, the weather will change, and some places will dry up. Trees use their roots to draw up rain water and release it through their leaves into the atmosphere as water vapor, a process known as transpiration. The water vapor forms clouds, which eventually fall as rain. It is estimated that the Amazon rainforests supply moisture for 50 percent of rainfall in the whole region. When trees are cut down, less rain and a drier climate may result. Dead trees also release carbon dioxide into the atmosphere and contribute to the greenhouse effect.

The greenhouse effect

Greenhouse gases, mainly CO_2, help regulate Earth's temperature by trapping some of the Sun's heat. For millions of years, a delicate balance of greenhouse gases kept temperatures stable. Over the past 200 years, the burning of **fossil fuels** has increased CO_2 levels and temperatures have risen. This is called global warming. Trees take in CO_2 as they grow, so the problem gets worse as forests are cleared. In addition, burning wood releases the carbon stored in trees. If the cleared forests are used to farm cattle, it makes matters worse. Cattle produce methane, another greenhouse gas.

Cameroon's Rainforests

Cameroon is a country in West Africa that has a total area of about 183,000 square miles (475,000 square kilometers). This small country contains 85,000 square miles (200,000 square kilometers) of tropical rainforest, one of the most important ecosystems in the world.

Components of the ecosystem

Africa is one of the few remaining places on Earth where rainforests are found. The Congo River, one of the largest rivers in the world, supplies plenty of water for the forests to flourish and grow. Animals like rhinoceroses, monkeys, elephants, antelopes, and deer live in the rainforests of Cameroon. Valuable trees such as mahogany and Pygeum can also be found here.

African elephants are an endangered species. Their habitat is at risk as the Cameroon rainforests are being cleared for timber.

Rainforest destruction

Until recently, Cameroon earned most of its income from oil exports and the rainforests were left more or less untouched. Oil prices and income fell, however, so the government started selling timber. Deforestation has increased and some 772 square miles (2,000 square kilometers) of forest are now lost every year. The huge Pygeum tree, *Prunus africana*, is very valuable because its bark contains a chemical used to treat chest pains and illnesses such as malaria and kidney disease. Local people cut down Pygeum trees and sell them. As a result, the trees are in danger of **extinction.**

Heavy machinery is often used to cut down trees and transport the timber out of the Cameroon rainforests.

The rainforest ecosystem in danger

As the Cameroon rainforests disappear, there will be less shelter and food for the animals living there. Road-building also fragments the forest and the exposed soil is easily washed away by rain. In addition, over 40 species of wildlife, including black rhinoceroses, gorillas, and elephants, may become extinct. Unless the rate of deforestation is controlled, this ecosystem may be totally destroyed.

Logging and bushmeat

Logging companies in Cameroon have greatly boosted the bushmeat trade. Bushmeat is wildlife that is hunted by people for food. Popular bushmeat includes gorillas, chimpanzees (*right*), elephants, and monkeys. As many of these animals are endangered, it has become illegal to hunt them. But logging companies have made it easy for poachers to get into forests by creating roads and tracks. The poachers then set small areas of forest on fire to scare the animals into specially laid traps.

Deforestation and Plants

As you have seen, forests are being cut down much faster than they can replace themselves. The areas where they grow are being used for cattle ranching, farming, and as places for people to live in. The result is that about 1,000 of the world's tree species are in danger of extinction. Most of these are only found in rainforests.

Valuable trees are disappearing

The rainforest is home to a huge variety of plants and animals. For example, about 170,000 different types of plants can be found in the tropics. In contrast, only 700 species of native plants are found in the United States and Canada put together. Many valuable species, especially tropical hardwoods, have been logged so heavily that they have become scarce. Brazilian rosewood is one of the best types of wood for making guitars and comes from the rainforest. Rosewood trees have become so rare that they are strictly protected. Mahogany wood is very popular for making furniture and, as a result, 70 percent of the world's mahogany trees have been felled. Mahogany trees in the Caribbean have almost disappeared. Since 2002, however, the felling of South American mahogany has been controlled.

The brightly colored fruit of an oil palm tree.

Losing beautiful and exotic plants

Other plants are also threatened by deforestation. Orchids are forest plants with beautiful, exotic flowers. As the forests disappear, orchid habitats are destroyed. As a result, many orchids have become rare. Pitcher plants are **carnivorous** plants that trap and digest insects in pitcher-shaped leaves. They can no longer be found in some forests of Southeast Asia.

The largest flower in the world, *Rafflesia arnoldii*, grows to about 3 feet (1 meter) across. It is only found in undisturbed rainforests in Indonesia and as these disappear, the flower faces extinction. Measures have been taken to protect the thirteen or so *Rafflesia* species, all of which are rare. In Malaysia, they are mainly found in conservation areas.

The Cochlioda vulcanica *orchid grows in northern Peru, Ecuador, and Bolivia.*

How rainforest plants are useful to humans

Forest plants are valuable to us in many ways. Many of our food crops, such as rice, banana, pineapple, corn, avocado, ginger, sugar, cinnamon, vanilla, and even cocoa, originally came from the rainforest. Many important drugs and medicines are found in the rainforest, too. The rosy periwinkle plant, a rainforest herb, contains chemicals that can help treat childhood leukemia. Scientists think different rainforest plants may contain chemicals to treat many other diseases. All these valuable plants will be lost once the forests disappear. The picture above shows an **indigenous** guide presenting a **medicinal** plant that grows in Karijini National Park in Western Australia.

Endangered Giants of the United States

Giant sequoias, which grow on high ground in North America, are the largest trees in the world. They were named in honor of a famous Native American leader, Sequoya, who invented the system of writing for the Cherokee language. A fully-grown giant sequoia can reach over 230 feet (80 meters) in height and about 100 feet (30 meters) in **circumference** at the base of its trunk. It takes the tree about 2,000 years to reach this size.

Redwood forests

One species of sequoia, *Sequoia sempervirens*, is called the redwood because of its cinnamon-brown bark. Redwoods grow in temperate forests with warm summers and cool winters. They mainly lie at the bottom of valleys along the Pacific Coast of California. More than 160 species of animals, including the marbled murrelet, the red-backed vole, and the spotted owl, live among the trees.

The huge red trunk of a giant sequoia in Yosemite National Park in California. Fully-grown giant sequoias can survive forest fires because their thick bark acts like a fireproof shell.

A section of redwood forest that has been cleared for timber.

A good source of timber

Unfortunately, the redwood tree is a very good source of timber. Its attractive color and natural resistance to decay and insects make the wood highly attractive to loggers and timber companies. A fully-grown tree can be about 390 feet (120 meters) tall and up to 30 feet (9 meters) in diameter at its base. 108,000 square feet (10,000 square meters) of redwood trees are worth as much as $800,000. Loggers use a very destructive method known as clear-cutting, where all the trees within a plot of land are cut down and removed. Without tree cover, the environment becomes drier and harsher. This affects other forest species, such as deer, black bears, and spotted owls.

What is left of the redwood forests?

Less than 2 percent of the original forests in the United States remain. Trees have been cleared to make way for agriculture, mining, oil-drilling activities, and the building of cities and industrial sites. This is also true of the majestic redwood forests. Once, 3,800 square miles (10,000 square kilometers) of redwood forest covered the western coast of the United States. Now, less than 4 percent remains. These magnificent trees need protection if they are to survive, as they take a very long time to mature. In the forest, a redwood tree may not produce seeds until it is 150 years old. With plenty of sunlight, however, seeds can appear on a tree after 20 years or so.

The fog belt

The only places where conditions are suitable for redwood trees to grow are about 20 to 35 miles (30 to 50 kilometers) away from the Pacific Coast. Along the southern Pacific Coast, there lies an area known as the fog belt. Although there is little rain, a thick fog covers the redwood forests almost all the time. When the fog condenses, it falls as very fine drizzle in the forests. The trees capture the moisture in the fog. It is this moisture that allows the redwoods to grow to such great sizes.

Deforestation and Animals

The lives of animals are closely linked to the plants in a forest. Animals help to pollinate the flowers of plants and to disperse their seeds. In return, they eat nectar and fruits. Carnivores in the forest, such as Sumatran tigers, feed on the smaller animals. When forests are cleared, animals lose their homes and food.

Animals in danger

Many animal species are in danger of becoming extinct along with plants, as their forest habitats disappear. Squirrel monkeys used to live in the forests of Costa Rica and Panama in Central America. Deforestation has forced these animals into small reserve areas in Costa Rica. The three-toed sloth, one of the slowest mammals in the rainforest, feeds on the leaves of the *Cecropia* tree and only produces one offspring a year. It does not survive very well outside the rainforest, not even in zoos. Now, conservationists have warned that this gentle animal is endangered as its habitat is being destroyed.

The Central American squirrel monkey weighs up to 2 pounds (1 kilogram) and lives in groups of 30 to 70 individuals. It rarely travels on the ground, preferring to spend most of its life in the trees. It depends on the trees for its food and to move from one place to another within the forest. As a result, any break in the forest caused by human activities can greatly reduce the size of its habitat.

A tiger suns itself in India.

Shrinking homes

The tiny geometric tortoise of South Africa has lost over 90 percent of its habitat. The few thousand tortoises that remain struggle to survive. They are surrounded by plants that they cannot eat and are frequently threatened by forest fires. In India, tigers have been under threat for many years. In the 1970s, Project Tiger banned the shooting of tigers for sport and the tiger population grew to about 4,000. They are now threatened again, this time by the destruction of their forest habitat. Huge dams are being built in forest areas to provide power and water for India's growing population. The Indian government plans to increase the area of the country covered by forest from 19 percent to 35 percent over the next 20 years, but it may be too late. Tigers may be almost extinct by 2010.

Vanishing animals

In 1981, there were around 1.2 million African elephants. By 1991, the number had reduced by about half and, by 2002, had fallen to as few as 300,000. About a third of the large tree species in Central Africa depend on elephants to spread their seeds, so even more deforestation may result. Another threatened animal is the mountain gorilla, which lives in the rainforest that straddles Rwanda, Uganda, and the Democratic Republic of the Congo. The gorilla population is coming under increasing threat because more and more of its forest habitat is being cleared for farming.

Using tarantulas to measure deforestation

Biologists are using tarantulas, the world's largest spiders, to measure the rate of deforestation in Belize. Redrump tarantulas live in dense forests, while cinnamon tarantulas prefer sunny clearings. Radio-tagging 50 spiders from each species and tracking their numbers will help measure the change in environment from forest to clearing. Tarantulas are particularly useful indicator species because they live for about 20 years in the same burrows.

The shy three-toed sloth makes its home in the canopy of the rainforest.

The European Mink

European mink used to be found in forests all over Europe. Now, this small mammal is only found in Belarus, France, Romania, Russia, and Spain. European mink have brown to black fur and partially webbed feet to help them swim and dive. They live near the banks of streams, rivers, and lakes in temperate forests. Their fur fetches a high price. A mink coat can cost up to $4,000. There may be less than 1,000 European mink left in all of Western Europe. In 1976, mink were declared a protected species, making it illegal for anyone to kill or trap them. The European mink population has continued to fall, however, and it is now one of the most endangered animals in the world.

The European mink often lives in a burrow, or hole in the ground, next to a river or stream.

The European mink is rarely found more than 328 feet (100 meters) from fresh water. It eats frogs, snails, crabs, fish, and insects.

Effects of human activities

European mink survive in France, but numbers have shrunk by about half over the past twenty years. Currently, they are found only in southwestern France. A major factor affecting their population is the clearing of forests for agriculture. As a result, the habitat of the European mink has been reduced. In addition, many streams have been drained to provide water for farmland. The remaining water supply of the mink has been polluted by fertilizers and pesticides from the farms. This drop in water quality is thought to be the main reason for the European mink's decline because its food supply is lost.

Accidental death

Scientists studied the causes of death of 88 European mink between 1965 and 1997. They found that about 75 percent were accidentally killed in traps set by hunters. A further 12 percent were killed by vehicles as they tried to cross the numerous roads that cut through the forests.

American versus European mink

The American mink was introduced into Europe in the mid-1920s so that it could be bred for its fur. Since then, American mink have escaped from fur farms across Europe and now live in the wild. This means they sometimes share the same habitat as European mink. American mink are more aggressive than European mink. As a result, American mink often **outcompete** European mink for food and space. This is another reason why the European mink population is threatened.

Deforestation and People

As well as plants and animals, some people make the forest their home. These indigenous populations have lived in the forests for thousands of years without upsetting the balance of the ecosystem. Around 140 million indigenous people are now at risk of losing their homes to deforestation.

Losing their homes and traditions

Forest dwellers have a very different lifestyle compared to urban or even rural people. They treat animals and plants in the forest with respect and take only what they need. One of the largest groups of Amazonian people still living as they have done for hundreds of years is the Yanomami. Although about 20,000 of them live in protected areas in Brazil and Venezuela, about a quarter have been affected by deforestation. Without the forest, they cannot continue their traditional lifestyle.

In Indonesia's rainforests, many villages have developed along river banks.

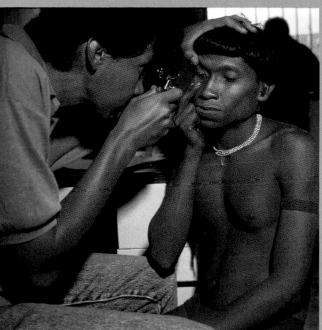

Disease and poverty

Besides losing their homes and food sources, forest populations are forced to accept a new way of life, often in poor conditions. As they have spent all their lives in the forest, they have little **immunity** and easily catch diseases in the outside world. In the last century, up to 90 groups of Amerindian peoples in Brazil died out from common diseases. Their cultures and languages vanished with them. In West Africa, many forests have been cleared to grow cocoa and oil palm and the indigenous peoples have had to move to new settlements on the outskirts of towns. Unfortunately, there are few jobs available, so the only option for many is to grow fruit to sell in markets or to tourists.

A Brazilian doctor examines a Yanomami.

Losing the air we breathe

Deforestation affects everyone, no matter where they live. Forests are important for the global climate. A growing tree removes carbon dioxide (CO_2) from the atmosphere that would otherwise add to global warming. Trees also release oxygen. Earth's rainforests alone produce about 40 percent of the planet's oxygen. The Amazon rainforest in South America is the largest rainforest in the world. It is often called the world's lungs because it produces more than 20 percent of Earth's oxygen. As long as forests are cut down on such a large scale, we will continue to lose this valuable source of oxygen.

Some people, like this family in Sri Lanka, build their homes in trees. Cutting down the forest destroys their traditional way of life.

Medicines from the rainforest

About a quarter of all our medicines come from rainforest plants. Curare is used as a poison on arrows by some Amazonian peoples. But in low doses, curare can help people who have multiple sclerosis or Parkinson's disease. Some cancer drugs are extracted from rainforest plants and a cure for AIDS may one day be found in the rainforest. If the forests are not protected, life-saving plants may be lost forever.

CASE STUDY

The Wanniyala-Aetto of Sri Lanka

For 18,000 years, the Wanniyala–Aetto lived in the tropical forests of Sri Lanka, hunting for meat and gathering plants and honey. They only took from the forest what they needed to feed their families. Experience taught them to farm small plots for a year or two, then leave them to recover for about seven years.

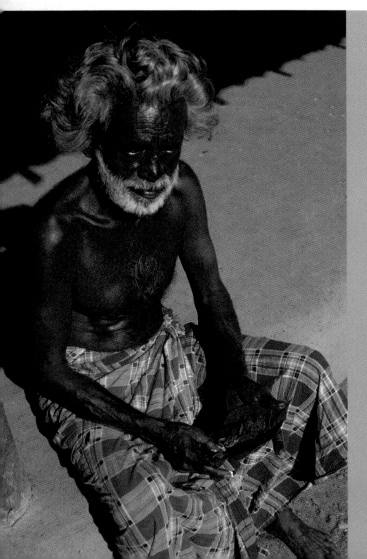

The threat from development

Over the past 50 years, the Sri Lankan government has removed this indigenous people from the forests. In 1955, the government built the Gal Oya Dam, which flooded the forest people's best hunting lands. Most of the population were resettled in specially built villages by the Sri Lankan government. But the Wanniyala–Aetto were used to living and moving about freely in the forest and could not adapt to this new lifestyle.

A Wanniyala-Aetto who has been forced to leave his forest home sits by the side of a road in Colombo in Sri Lanka. The Wanniyala-Aetto who now live in Sri Lankan cities are usually jobless because they do not have the skills to work in an urban environment.

Invasion of other people

In 1977, the government decided to clear more forest to build a hydroelectric dam across the largest river in the country, the Mahaweli Ganga. During the project, 42 square miles (110 square kilometers) of the Wanniyala–Aetto's last remaining hunting grounds were cleared. Thousands of settlers moved in to grow rice on the cleared land and more indigenous people were resettled.

Hydroelectric dams like this one provide about two-thirds of Sri Lanka's electricity. Dam-building, however, can have a devastating effect on the neighboring environment. It not only damages surrounding forests but also displaces people living in nearby areas, destroying their homes and traditional way of life.

Three Wanniyala-Aetto stand holding traditional bows and arrows.

A national park — the final blow

In 1983, the government turned the remaining forest into a national park. The last few Wanniyala–Aetto were removed from their forest homes and told it was illegal for them to return. Today fewer than 2,500 survive. As a result of their changed lifestyle, many suffer from health problems such as depression, obesity, and diabetes.

Return to the forest — good news?

In 1998, the Sri Lankan government finally gave in to pressure from international campaigning and agreed that the Wanniyala–Aetto could return to live in the forest, starting with a group of 50. In practice, however, the people are still fined or imprisoned for poaching when they hunt in their traditional way.

The Western diet — bad news

Hunter-gatherers like the Wanniyala–Aetto have not been able to adjust to a steady food supply. Over thousands of years, their bodies have adapted to store as much fat as possible to get them through times when food was scarce. Since switching to a high-fat, Western-style diet, many have become obese. Obesity can lead to many health problems, including heart disease and diabetes.

The World Wildlife Fund

The World Wildlife Fund (WWF) was founded in 1961 to raise money for conservation. From the beginning it was an international organization. Although its headquarters was in Switzerland, its **founders** realized that the most effective way to raise funds and tell people about the need for conservation was to set up offices in many different countries.

Focus on forests

In 1996, the WWF launched its Forests for Life Campaign. The theme is "Protect, Manage, and Restore." WWF works to protect the world's remaining forests and to make sure that they are properly managed. It also tries to restore land that was once forest to its original state. The WWF believes illegal logging, conversion of forests to plantation cropland, forest fires, and climate changes are the worst threats to forests.

Scientists working with the WWF examine the condition of forests in Westphalia, Germany.

The oil palm threat

Over the past 20 years, more than 1.2 million square miles (3 million square kilometers) of tropical forest, an area larger than India, have been cleared for agriculture, mining, and urban development. Over the next 25 years, a similar amount of forest is likely to be lost. Oil palm, which is grown to produce vegetable oils, is the most common agricultural crop. The WWF works with the producers of oil palm in countries such as Indonesia to manage land use, preserve the most important parts of the forest, and use the cleared land efficiently.

An oil palm tree growing on deforested land on the island of Sumatra in Indonesia.

The WWF tackles illegal logging

Illegal logging is big business all over the world. The WWF campaigns to make governments, industries, and consumers aware of how illegal logging destroys the forest ecosystem. It also encourages the use of timber certification and tracking. This involves following wood from the forest until it is made into a finished product. Certified timber or wood products often carry a product label. This label lets industries and consumers know that the timber or wood product originally came from a **sustainable** forested area.

Saving the panda's habitat

The giant panda is the symbol of the WWF. The organization is supporting a 30-member team to protect and monitor 198 square miles (512 square kilometers) of forest in the Qinling Mountains of China, one of the few remaining natural habitats of the giant panda. The WWF is also working with the local government to make sure tourism does not destroy conservation efforts.

Tasmania's Forest Cycle

A river flowing through the Tarkine, the largest area of temperate rainforest in Australia. About 70 percent of the Tarkine in northwestern Tasmania is covered with rainforest.

A logging train transports logs to a processing factory in Bell Bay in northern Tasmania, where the logs will be turned into wood chips. The wood chip industry provides very few jobs for Tasmanians. The number of Tasmanians employed in the wood and paper industries dropped from 5,600 in 1991 to 3,827 in 1996 and is still falling.

Tasmania has the largest area of temperate rainforest in Australia. Unlike tropical rainforests, it consists mainly of eucalyptus trees. These can grow very tall: the tallest eucalyptus ever recorded is 330 feet (101 meters) high.

The plight of the forest

Tasmanian forests have problems as bad as those of the Amazon rainforests. An average of 100 square miles (260 square kilometers) of forest is felled every year. About three-quarters of this is clear-cut and burned, destroying the entire ecosystem. Up to 90 percent of the wood is exported as wood chips, mainly to Japan, where it is used to make paper. Tasmania exports more wood chips than all the other Australian states put together.

The Forest Cycle

More than 80 percent of Tasmanians are against the wood chip industry, even though it is supported by the taxes they pay. Many groups and societies are helping to fight commercial logging. In 1999, and again in 2000, a group of **protesters** cycled 372 miles (600 kilometers) across Tasmania in the middle of winter with the slogan, "For the forests, the jobs, the community." The cyclists visited different communities to persuade people to get involved in protecting the forests.

A cyclist on the Tasmanian Trail, which formed part of the Forest Cycle.

Spreading the message

The aim of the cyclists was to spread the message that commercial logging and burning the forests to clear land for agriculture are not good for the environment. This is because both of these actions do not promote sustainable development. Sustainable development satisfies present human needs for water, land, and food without destroying these resources for future generations.

Animals of the Tasmanian forest

Many unique animals are dying out as they lose their forest homes. The spotted-tail quoll (*right*) is a carnivorous mammal that comes out mainly at night. The males can grow to 51 inches (130 centimeters) long and weigh about 9 pounds (4 kilograms). They eat rats, reptiles, and insects. Quolls have almost died out in mainland Australia and are rare in Tasmania. The Tasmanian wedge-tailed eagle is a massive bird with a wingspan of up to 7 feet (2.2 meters). They are very shy and desert their nests if they are disturbed. Clearing trees has left only 130 breeding pairs of wedge-tailed eagles, which are now listed as an endangered species.

Saving Trees: India's Chipko Movement

India's most successful **conservation movement** began in the Himalayas in the 1970s. A group of hill tribes started a peaceful protest against further clearing of their highland forests. These Himalayan villagers formed circles around the trees, shielding them from lumberjacks and bulldozers. The movement spread across India and became known as the Chipko Movement. *Chipko* is the Hindi word for "embrace."

*Sunderlal Bahuguna is an important member of the Chipko Movement. He is known as "the **mahatma** of India's forests."*

Taking action!

Sunderlal Bahuguna, an Indian activist and philosopher, focused worldwide attention on India's endangered forests. From 1981 to 1983, he walked a distance of about 3,100 miles (5,000 kilometers) through the Himalayas, seeing how development projects such as dams caused damage to the environment. He sent a report of his findings to the United Nations. In 1996 and 1997, Sunderlal Bahuguna fasted for more than 90 days to protest against the building of a dam across the Ganges River. He said that the dam would flood the surrounding forest and destroy the homes of thousands of villagers.

Extensive logging has destroyed many forests in India.

Protecting the highland forests

In 1980, India's prime minister, Indira Gandhi, placed a ban on cutting down highland trees. The government also planted new trees to provide food and fuel for the hill tribes. Respect for the environment increased in the 1990s, and the government introduced laws to reduce pollution. Today Chipko supporters continue to try and prevent further deforestation in India.

Lifelong friends

To some of India's tribal people, trees are more than a source of food and fuel. They represent life itself. Whenever a child is born, a tree is planted in the child's name. The tree grows with the child and the two enjoy a close, lifelong relationship. As the tree bears fruit and provides for the child, the child's duty is to protect the tree.

Inspired by history and culture

The Chipko Movement really began in the 18th century, when hundreds of members of an Indian tribe, the Bishnoi, died to save their khejari forest. The khejari (*right*) is a tree that provides shade and food in a harsh desert. It is **sacred** to the Bishnoi people. When the king of Jodhpur (a kingdom in north-western India) sent his axemen to collect timber from a Bishnoi village, a brave woman named Amrita Devi threw herself in front of the first threatened tree. She was killed by the king's men, but her daughters and hundreds of Bishnoi tribespeople followed her example. They hugged the trees and died with them. Today, an annual fair remembers the sacrifice of the Bishnoi people. Their actions inspired the modern Chipko Movement.

Positive Action

Forests are important to wildlife, indigenous peoples, and even to people who live in cities or other countries. As the world's population grows, we will need more land, energy, and food. Most of these resources will come from forests. More trees will be cut down, more land will be cleared for farms and buildings, and more roads will be built. What can we do to stop all the forests from disappearing?

Using less

The world will always need wood products and trees will always be cut down. However, trees can be saved if people use fewer wood products by using recycled paper, for example. This is good for the environment in other ways: making recycled paper uses 61 percent less water and produces 71 percent less air pollution than making new paper from trees.

These teenagers have volunteered to bundle newspapers at a paper recycling center in Great Britain. Great Britain recycled 65.1 percent of newspapers printed in the country in 2002. The percentage of newspapers recycled in Australia and the United States for the same year was 72.8 percent and 71.2 percent, respectively.

More sustainable forestry

It is possible to manage forestry so that it is less destructive. Sustainable resources are given time to renew themselves. In the case of forests, there are several measures that can be taken. Logging companies can be made to cut down only trees above a certain size and only a certain number of trees per area of forest. The use of heavy machinery can be limited, and the number of roads made into the forest controlled. Trees can even be removed from forests by helicopter, although this is very expensive.

These tree saplings have been planted on land that was once cleared for agriculture in Great Britain.

Local people benefit, too

The interests of local people are part of **sustainable forestry.** If they are provided with food and a means of making a living, people do not need to clear forests to grow crops. Villagers can be encouraged to plant fruit trees for food. The growth of ecotourism provides employment and gives local people a good reason to conserve their forests.

Taman Negara is Malaysia's largest national park and an important ecotourist destination. About 60,000 tourists visit the park every year.

In a nutshell

Forests are threatened because:
- they are clear-cut to provide land for cattle ranches, agricultural activities, towns, and cities
- they are cut down to provide timber for building and manufacturing and wood pulp for making paper
- they are destroyed by pollution and acid rain

Forests should be conserved because:
- they help to control the climate by absorbing carbon dioxide and creating rainfall
- they provide oxygen for people to breathe
- they are important habitats for plants, animals, and indigenous peoples
- they provide plants that have medicinal properties
- they provide valuable resources, such as wood for timber and furniture

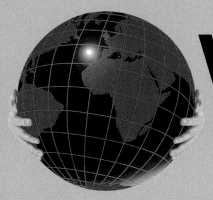

What Can I Do?

Everyone can help to save the forests, including you. Here are some ways you can help.

Recycle, reuse, reduce

- Persuade your parents not to buy tropical rainforest products such as mahogany furniture without Forest Stewardship Council (FSC) labels. These labels let people know that the wood has come from a well-managed forest.

- Do not waste paper. Save trees by writing on both sides of a sheet of paper whenever you can. Set up recycling bins in your home and classroom to collect unwanted paper that can still be used. Reuse the paper to practice drawing or to make notes. Take old newspapers to recycling centers.

- Use recycled paper or paper made from non-tree fibers, such as hemp.

- Choose products that have little or no packaging. Take your own reusable bags when shopping instead of accepting paper bags from stores.

- Stop junk mail coming into your home. Write to Mail Preference Service, PO Box 643, Carmel NY 10512, and tell them that you do not wish to receive such mail. This will reduce your family's junk mail by up to 75 percent, saving up to 1.5 trees per person per year.

These people in Barcelona in Spain are protesting against the use of illegal wood from African rainforests. They are also campaigning for the use of wood products that have FSC labels.

These children in the Solomon Islands are protesting against the destruction of their forest for mining activities.

Plan and plant trees

To celebrate World Forestry Day on March 21, why not plant a tree?

- Select a suitable area of land within your school grounds.
- Clear away any grass or weeds already growing on the site.
- Buy a tree seedling from a local garden center.
- Within the selected piece of land, dig a hole larger than the seedling. Then pour water into the hole.
- Carefully lift the seedling out of its container and place it gently into the hole. Be careful not to damage the roots.
- Fill the space around the seedling with soil, firmly pressing down the soil.
- Cut a hole in a piece of folded newspaper. Then open up the newspaper and place the hole in the paper over the seedling.
- Put small stones on the four corners of the paper to stop it from blowing away. The paper will protect the seedling from any weeds and from the wind.

Learn about your planet and environment

- Learn more about the environment you live in and the forests around your home from newspapers, books, and websites.
- Work with your classmates to list all the forest products in your home, school, and other places. Remember to include foods and medicines. Then try to find out which types of forests these products have come from. This will make you more aware of how forests affect your everyday life.

Get involved

- Join an organization that works to protect forests, such as the World Wildlife Fund (http://panda.org).

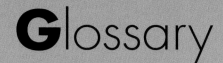 **G**lossary

acid rain rain containing dissolved sulfur dioxide and nitrogen oxides

acidic substance with a sour taste. Strong acids can dissolve even metal.

biodiversity different plant and animal species present in a given area

canopy covering; in a forest, it is created by the highest leaves and branches of trees

carnivorous meat-eating; carnivores are animals that eat other animals

chlorophyll green pigment needed by plants to trap light energy and make food

circumference outer boundary, especially of a circle

clear-cut cut down all the trees in one area

compact press together closely

coniferous trees that grow cones

conservation movement large group of people who protect something from harm or prevent wasteful use of resources

deciduous trees that lose their leaves in winter

decompose break down and decay

deforestation removal of forests; forests may be removed as a source of timber, to clear the land for farms or cities, or by natural processes

dormant state of rest and inactivity; dormant seeds do not grow for a period so as to survive harsh environmental conditions such as winter

ecosystem community of plants and animals in a physical environment

evergreen trees that have green leaves all year

exporter person or company that transports goods to other countries

extinct exists no more; dead

fossil fuel fuel derived from the fossilized remains of plants and animals. Examples of fossil fuels are coal and oil.

founder person who establishes a group or community

gap open space; in the forest, a gap is created when trees fall

germinate grow from a seed into a young plant or seedling

global warming rise in global temperature caused by increasing amounts of greenhouse gases, such as carbon dioxide, in the atmosphere. The climate change can affect daily life and agriculture.

herb non-woody, small plant such as a fern or wild ginger

hunter-gatherer person who gets food by hunting, fishing, or looking for it in the wild

immunity resistance to a particular disease, usually gained by vaccination or catching the disease in childhood

indicator species animals and plants that only live in particular environments, due to conditions such as rainfall and sunlight

indigenous belongs naturally to a particular area

infertile has limited nutrients; infertile soil cannot be used for agriculture

mahatma person who is highly respected for his/her wisdom

medicinal having the properties of a medicine

migratory traveling from one habitat to another in order to mate or find food

monitor see and record

nutrient substance required by a living thing for growth and energy. Plants need carbon dioxide and water, as well as nitrogen and magnesium, which can often be obtained from the soil.

outcompete successfully defeat

photosynthesize use light energy to make food from carbon dioxide and water. Only green plants photosynthesize because they have chlorophyll to trap light energy.

plot measured area of land

pollinate transfer pollen from the stamen (male part) to the ovule (female part) of a plant. This process is important for coniferous and flowering plants to reproduce.

primary forest natural, original forest. This is not a forest planted by humans or one that grows in a patch of forest that was previously cleared.

protester person who objects to something

sacred holy; regarded with respect

secondary forest forest that replaces the land after a primary forest is cleared

sediment fine material like dust that is deposited by winds, glaciers, and rivers and then settles on the ocean bed

sustainable able to renew itself

sustainable forestry proper use of forests to meet our needs while ensuring that they will still be around in the future

temperate climatic zone characterized by mild weather and distinct seasons

topsoil fertile, upper layer of soil. This layer contains the nutrients that plants need to grow well.

Further Reading

Books:

Cefrey, Holly. *Coniferous Forests*. New York:
Rosen Publishing, 2003.

Dalgleish, Sharon. *Protecting Forests*. Broomall,
Penn.: Chelsea House, 2003.

George, Michael. *Rainforests: Endangered Jewels*.
Mankato, Minn.: The Creative Company, 2003.

Greeley, August. *Fading Forests: The Destruction of
Our Rainforests*. New York: Rosen Publishing, 2003.

MacMillan, Diane. *Life in a Deciduous Forest*.
Minneapolis, Minn.: Lerner Publishing, 2003.

Parker, Janice (ed.). *The Disappearing Forests*.
North Mankato, Minn.: Smart Apple Media, 2002.

Rapp, Valerie. *Life in an Old Growth Forest*.
Minneapolis, Minn.: Lerner Publishing, 2002.

Woodward, John. *Temperate Forests*. Chicago:
Raintree Publishers, 2002.

Videos:

All about Forest Ecosystems. Ecosystems for Children
series, Schlessinger Media (2001)

How They Make Paper. Did You Ever Wonder? series,
FilmWest Associates (1998)

Jungle. Eyewitness series, DK Publishing (1995)

Rainforest Biomes. Biomes of the World in Action
series, Schlessinger Media (2001)

Websites:

Amazon Interactive
http://www.eduweb.com/amazon.html

Endangered Animals Centre
http://worldkids.net/eac/

Environmental Explorers' Club
http://www.epa.gov/kids/

Network for Healthy Living and a Healthy Planet
http://www.care2.com

Recycle City
http://www.epa.gov/recyclecity

Organizations:

Australian Conservation Foundation
Floor 1, 60 Leicester Street
Carlton
Victoria 3053
Australia
Phone: (03) 9345 1111
Fax: (03) 9345 1166
http://www.acfonline.org.au/

Defenders of Wildlife
National Headquarters
1130 17th Street, NW
Washington, DC 20030
Phone: (202) 682 9400
http://www.defenders.org/

Rainforest Alliance
Suite 500
665 Broadway
New York, NY 10012
Phone: 212 677 1900
http://www.rainforest-alliance.org/

The World Wide Fund for Nature
WWF-UK
Panda House, Weyside Park
Godalming, Surrey GU7 1XR
Great Britain
Phone: 1483 426 444; 1483 426 409
http://www.wwf-uk.org

Index